VISIONS OF WANDERLUST

the world of travel photography

the very best of the first five years of the
Wanderlust Travel Photo of the Year competition

Published by Wanderlust Publications Ltd.
Leworth Place, Mellor Walk, Bachelors Acre,
Windsor, SL4 1EB U.K.

Tel: +44 (0)1753 620426
Fax: +44 (0)1753 620474

www.wanderlust.co.uk
Email: info@wanderlust.co.uk

Editors: Lyn Hughes & Paul Morrison
Designer: Paraic Maddock
Sub-editor: Lizzie Kendon
Co-ordinator: Sam Wright

Wanderlust

ISBN 0-9540926-0-0

Printed in Italy by EuroLitho

Contents

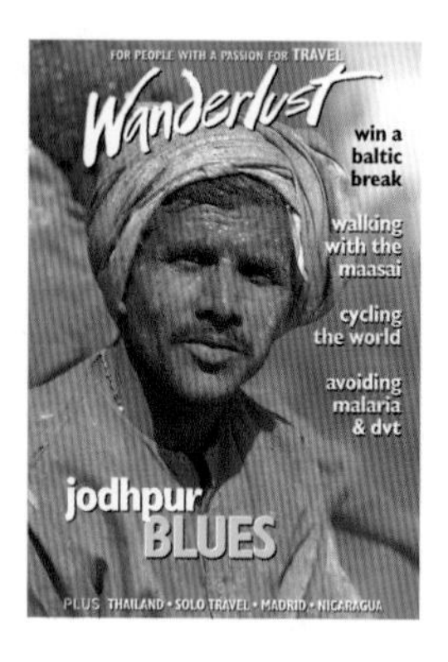

Wanderlust

THE MAGAZINE

Wanderlust was launched in 1993, by Paul Morrison and Lyn Hughes. It has since become the UK's leading specialist travel magazine, with its hallmark mix of inspirational reporting and impartial information. Top-class photography has been a feature of the magazine from the start, aiming to show the world as it is, rather than how we might like it to be.

Wanderlust

THE PHOTO COMPETITION

The competition is launched each September and runs to the end of the year. Entry is open to any amateur photographer with a UK address. The panel of judges draws up a shortlist of entries, which are displayed at *Destinations* – the UK's leading travel and holiday show. It is here that the final judging and presentations take place. Overall winners go on a photographic commission for *Wanderlust*, the recent hosts being Namibia and Thailand.

For details on entering check out the October/November or December/January issues of *Wanderlust*, or log on to www.wanderlust.co.uk.

THANKS

The success of the *Wanderlust Travel Photo of the Year* competition has been due to the support of a number of individuals and organisations, who have shared our enthusiasm for showcasing the photographic talents of our readers.

Destinations has provided the ideal venue every year for an exhibition of the finalists, and the nerve-wracking awards ceremony. Thanks to the 'Desties' team.

Our thanks must go to *The Independent*, and particularly travel editor Simon Calder, for all his encouragement and support. In 2000 *The Daily Telegraph* came on board as media sponsors, so a thank you too to the team there, especially Graham Boynton and Avril O'Reilly.

Our gratitude must also go out to the various sponsors over the years, who have offered such excellent prizes for the competition winners, especially: Rohan, Namibia Tourism, Tourism Authority of Thailand (Chris Lee in particular), Canon, Nikon and Billingham.

To the various judges and helpers, especially Jack Jackson and Geoffrey Roy, another big thanks. And last, but not least, the biggest thank you goes to all those people who have entered the competition since its launch, making it the success that it is. We hope you'll feel encouraged by this selection to get out there again and submit more entries.

"I can't believe they're not professionals"

is the typical response to the annual exhibition of the finalists in the Wanderlust Travel Photo of the Year. Now, with this opportunity to look back on the first five years of the competition, the myth that only a pro can take a decent travel photo is well and truly exploded. In fact, there's something about a vision of the world seen through the eyes of a true traveller that brings a freshness and honesty to the images.

These are the visions we present here – images of the world as it is, not ones destined for corporate calendars or glossy brochures, but intended for the pleasure of the people who took them. They capture the sense of discovery that travellers experience when propelled away from their daily routines into cultures and landscapes which re-awaken the senses.

The competition began in 1996, prompted by the high standard of photographs we were receiving from the readers of Wanderlust magazine. To keep it a readers' affair we placed a restriction that prevented professional photographers from entering, and it soon became the UK's biggest travel photography competition for amateurs.

Since then, the Wanderlust office has been deluged each winter with thousands of envelopes containing the favourite travel photographs of readers from all walks of life: teachers and students, debt collectors and social workers, actors and air-traffic controllers.

We'd be doing these travellers a great disservice, however, by suggesting that the photos that make it to the final shortlist each year are of less than professional quality. Indeed, the pros who have helped us judge the contest over the years have been unanimous in their praise, and not a little envious. Although the equipment used has varied from happy-snappies through to Hasselblads, the standard of finalists' photos has been consistently excellent, with genuine talent on show.

With prize commissions on offer (recent winners have jetted off to Namibia and Thailand), some of the finalists have not surprisingly used their success as a springboard to a new career in photography. Most, however, are content with a moment of glory and rely on a more regular source of income to fund their next overseas adventure.

It is a passion for travel, shared by these photographers, that ensures a fresh crop of new images every year. It also helps explain why the competition continues to grow in scale and standard. Judge for yourself in this selection of the best photographs from the first five years. Perhaps after seeing these you'll feel inspired to enter next time.

Lyn Hughes & Paul Morrison

[*in the city*] 1

Frank Tyler Havana, Cuba

A local man with his prized 1951 Chevrolet Styleline sedan on the Malecón in the late afternoon.

Robert Gray New York, USA

The Statue of Liberty, taken in the early morning from the pedestal, on a special trip with my eight-year-old daughter, Liberty.

Early Sunday morning on a subway between Brooklyn and Manhattan.

Simon Hadley New York, USA

Steven Blackburn San Francisco, USA

We arrived in San Francisco on a misty winter morning. This homeless man was keen to swap a photo for some cigarettes. We chatted a bit – he was a really **nice guy.**

These smiling girls are pulling away from a wedding they have just attended on the Prado, a major avenue through central Havana. I shot just this one frame.

Kris Allan Havana, Cuba

Nigel Craig Musée D'Orsay, Paris

This was very much a grab shot, taken in the autumn of 1999. What attracted me was the young couple looking 'through' the clock with the Paris skyline behind. It only occurred to me later that they could be looking towards the approaching new millennium.

Lynn Frieda Phnom Penh, Cambodia

Two small boys

pause along the promenade at the confluence of the Mekong and Tonlé Sap rivers.

Graffiti wall.

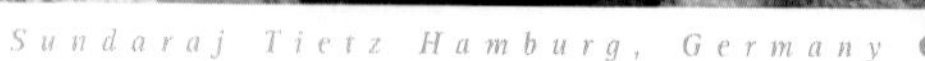

Sundaraj Tietz Hamburg, Germany

Kevin Adlard Havana, Cuba

A young boy sitting on the running-board of his father's **derelict car** just after a rain storm.

John Hulme Chiang Mai, Thailand

Playing **cards** backstage with the *katoey* (transvestite) performers of the Blue Moon Theatre.

Piers Newbery Manhattan, New York, USA

Workers painting an advertisement mural near Times Square.

Guy Moberly Belém, Brazil

Despite his deformities this man exuded an air of

calm, dignity

and resignation.

I spoke to him for a week before lying down on the pavement and taking this shot.

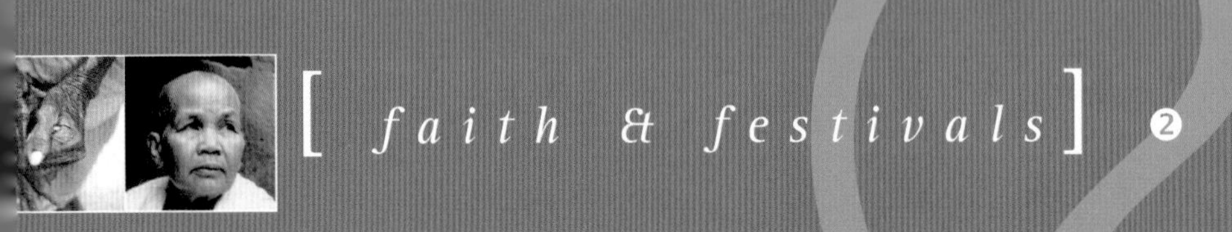

2

[*faith & festivals*] 2

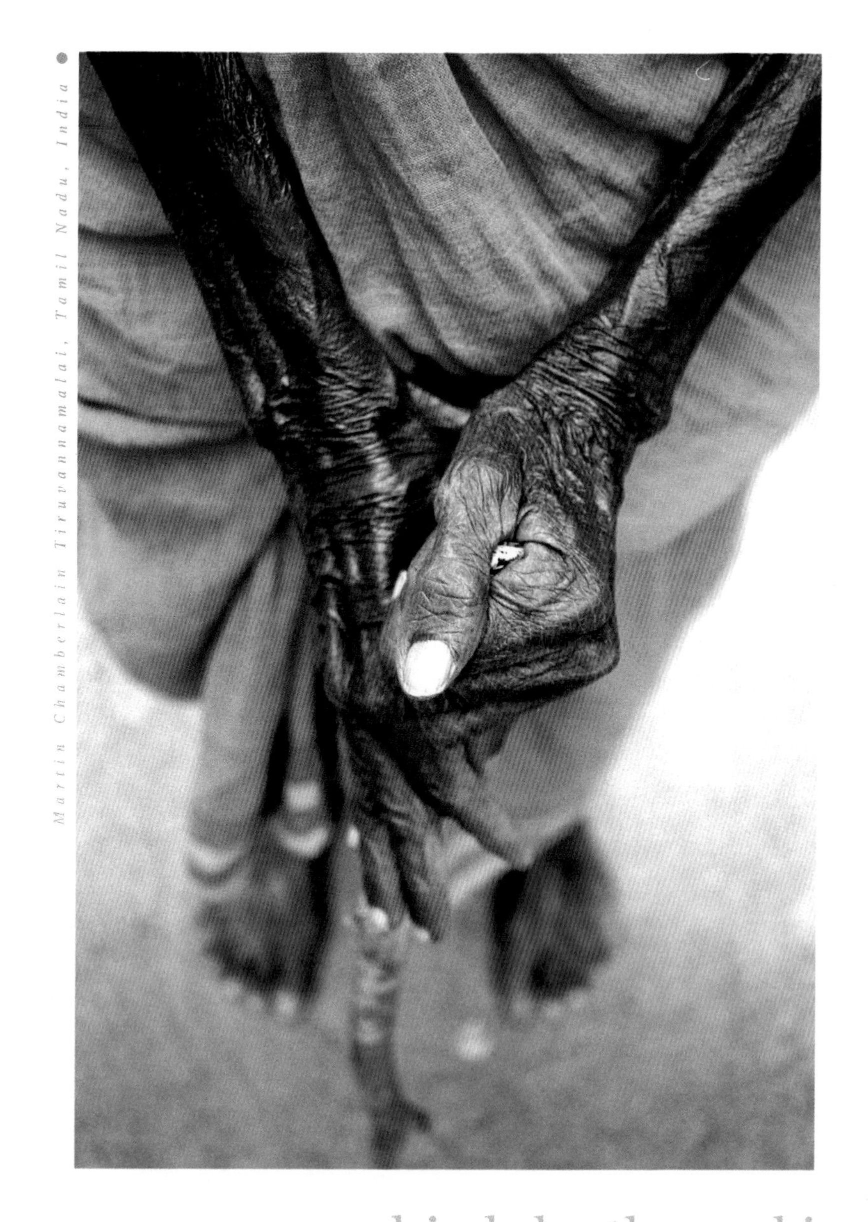

Martin Chamberlain Tiruvannamalai, Tamil Nadu, India

I met this very old lady with dark, sun-dried, leathery skin. After asking her permission, I took a couple of photographs of her full length but it was really her hands on the walking stick that I wanted to capture.

At a Tibetan monastery, these students were **waiting at the entrance** to their temple.

Peter Hamilton Pokhara, Nepal

Lynn Frieda Angkor Wat, Cambodia

An elderly nun offers guests **incense** in the doorway to one of Angkor's ancient monuments.

Toni Greaves Paro, Bhutan

Two young Buddhist monks watch the Paro Festival, celebrated each spring in honour of Guru Rimpoche. It is a major social gathering where everyone dresses in their finest clothing and jewellery. During part of the festival citizens and monks perform dances to bless and protect onlookers.

Jim Sherwood Seville, Spain ●

After a procession throughout the previous night to the cathedral, on the morning of **Good Friday** the brotherhood (cofradia) of the Church of Santa Ana were close to reaching the church.

During the annual Holi festival I followed the procession through the streets, among the hordes of people and **flying coloured paint**. Moments after taking this photo I was almost mown down by three camels.

Timothy Rogers Udaipur, India ●

Jeremy Hunter Co. Kerry, Ireland

It was a **stormy** day at Inch Bay and pouring with rain. The nuns were parked in a minibus on the sand, and I knew that when the rain stopped they would surely go for a **walk along the beach.**

This group was waiting for a procession

to pass. The boy with the goldfish caught my eye.

Jim Sherwood Ubud, Bali, Indonesia

Diane Barker Kathmandu, Nepal

The two nuns in the photo were wonderfully playful and were very keen to have their photos taken. Like most Tibetans they had a great **sense of fun** and were pulling faces.

At a Kali temple in Amber, near Jaipur, I witnessed the ceremony of chudakarma – the first tonsure performed on the child's first birthday. The cut hair is offered to Kali; this is a very important religious ceremony for the whole family.

Alex Psirides Rajasthan, India

Jessica Loeb Isfahan, Iran

Masjed-é Emam. The mosque was empty save for these ladies chatting in the sunlight.

The saffron-coloured robe of the

Buddha

stood out instantly against the overcast

sky and the grey towers of the Bayon.

Jamie Marshall Angkor Thom, Cambodia

David Watts Tay Ninh, Vietnam

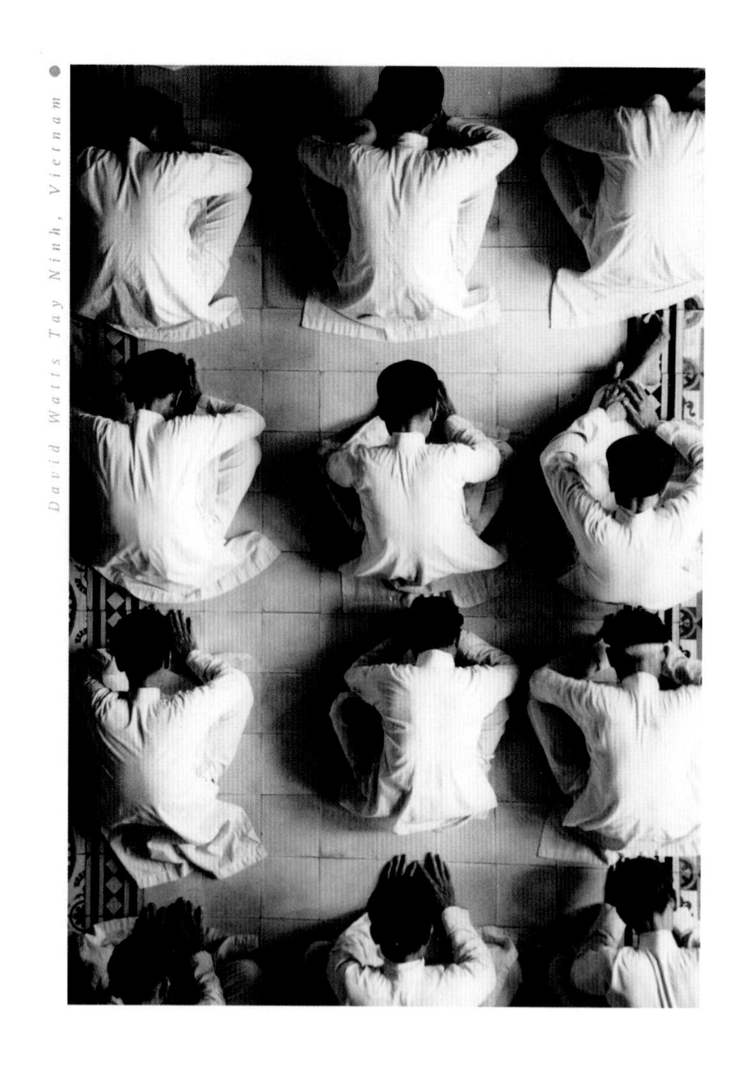

'God's View' – Caodai Great Temple. Worshippers gather at midnight, midday and 6am and 6pm for prayer and visitors can watch the whole scene from the first floor balcony.

Paul Gallagher Himachal Pradesh, Northern India

Tibetan Buddhist Monks. This photograph was taken during a candle-lit vigil against Chinese repression in Tibet. I tried to capture the dignity, peace and compassion shown by Tibetan monks in campaigning for a free country.

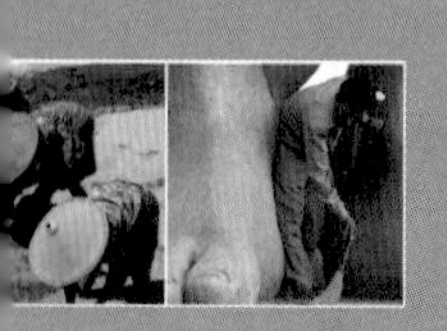

[*at work*] 3

The stamina of these villagers transplanting **rice** was a marvel; it was Ramadan yet they still managed to work from very early **morning** until **dusk** and beyond.

Dave Winter Sapit, Lombok, Indonesia

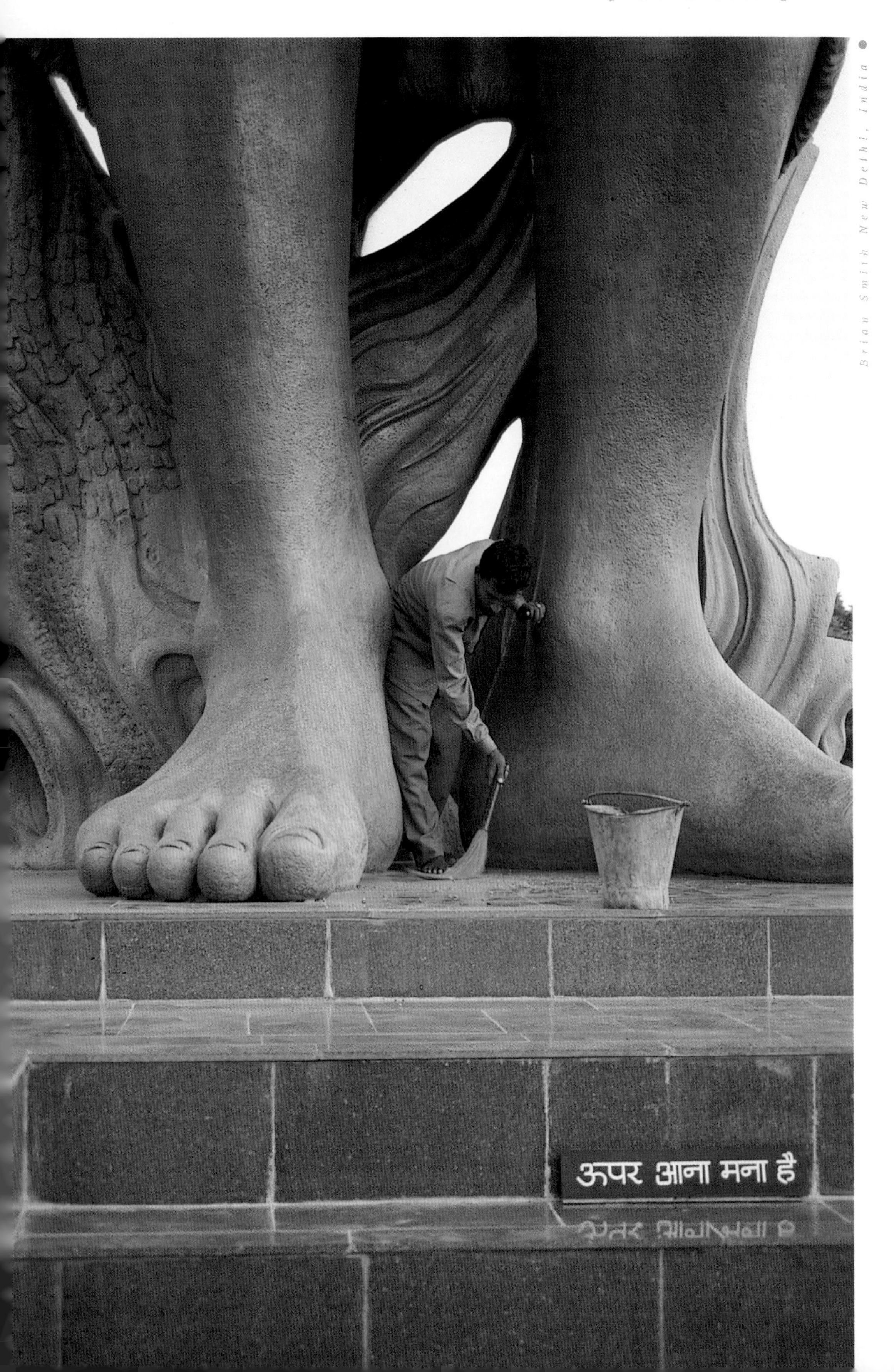

Brian Smith New Delhi, India

The statue is of the

Hindu god Siva.

The worker sweeping around

the statue's feet

illustrates its vast scale.

Richard Stephens Southern India

Driver and fireman on a steam locomotive.

Dave Winter Isfahan, Iran

Around midday, shafts of light come streaming through the holes in the roof of this old caravanserai. The shaft of light on the bicycle was enhanced by the porter arriving pulling a hand-cart.

John Millen Southern Nepal

These two porters were resting on their 'T' braced walking sticks after crossing a river. They were on their way to market carrying onions and potatoes and the odd pot for cooking along the way.

Laurence Winter Pinar del Río, Cuba

Sugar-cane workers.

There's a certain **timeless** quality to this image – it could have been taken any time in the past 50 years.

Steve Rowley Atlantic Ocean, 500 miles east of Antigua

Trimming the topsail.

Redwoods being **felled**

at Redwood College student campus.

Robert Nichol Eureka, California, USA

Sue Moore Rajasthan, India

Street **barber**

in Bikaner.

Dave Winter Xinjiang province, China

This picture was taken during

one of several visits I have made to the

town of Kashgar.

The famous Sunday Market is a real slice of central

Asian life. I defy anyone not to get great pictures here.

Brian Bowles Singapore

One evening I chanced upon a

Chinese opera

theatre who were due to perform in a couple of hours. The performers were extremely friendly and very happy to let me wander backstage and photograph them.

[*earth, air, fire & water*] 4

I spent five hours in Upper

Antelope Canyon taking images and

immersing myself in its wonder,

exquisite
texture

and colours.

Dr Tejas Udani Arizona, USA

Vanessa Latford Thingvellir National Park, Iceland

It was a very **showery day**

in Thingvellir National Park and not a member

of our group could resist this beautiful scene.

Martin Bradley El Calafate, Patagonia, Argentina

Dusty gravel-topped roads and unpredictable weather are

typical of this region, which retains something of a

wild west frontier atmosphere.

Ian Cameron Zanzibar

At the north-east tip of the island, we stumbled across a **deserted beach**.

When the red-sailed dhow passed by I knew I had my shot.

George Carmichael has been a close friend for 40 years and he adopted walking as therapy after heart problems. Blencathra is one of the northern fells and we climbed via the spectacular

Sharp Edge.

Bert Whalley Blencathra, Cumbria Lake District

Mike Morton Bryce Canyon, USA

The first morning we woke early to find no sun.
On the second morning it was **perfect.**

In 2000 the south-east crater of **Mount Etna** erupted every few days. These dramatic events were usually short-lived, but nevertheless spectacular. In June I was lucky enough to see two of these eruptions. The biggest lava fountain ever filmed on Etna reared 850m above the crater – we were only 500m away. It was **a little hot.**

Jeremy Bishop Mount Etna, Sicily

Tim Lynch Okavango Delta, Botswana

We had paddled for a day in mokoro – dugout canoes. The scene wasn't as tranquil as it looks – a hippo, with what sounded like a severe digestive problem, was rumbling nearby.

Sue O'Connell Muscat, Oman

I took this shot from the Qurm Heights on a December afternoon. For a few short moments, the light illuminating the sea and shoreline was magical.

Mike Surowiak San Francisco, California, USA ●

At **sunrise**, the Golden Gate Bridge rose out of the fog-filled bay.

Leo Palmer Dead Vlei, Namibia

An old pan with skeletons of dead acacia trees deprived of water when the river changed course. Some of the trees are over 500 years old.

Sand dune at the edge of the Sahara. Shot during the early morning light to capture the low sun angle and the shadows.

Roderick Macmillan Merzouga, Morocco

Shaun Laws Annapurna Region, Nepal

I was admiring the enormity of

Annapurna at sunrise

when a group of trekkers stepped into the frame and gave a sense of scale to the picture.

Jon Christie Gokyo Ri, Nepal

Tibetan prayer flags

at the summit of Gokyo Ri looking over the Ngozumpa Glacier and Gokyo village.

Gerry Rusbridge Ladakh, North India

Prayer flags fluttering at a fort above Leh, the capital of Ladakh.

In the background lies the Zanskar mountain range.

Jonathan Gregson Jökulsárlón, Iceland

Standing on the jetty, the cold silence was broken only by the intermittent crashing of ice breaking free from the glacier.

Ron Tear Brecon Beacons, Wales

We had just reached the summit of Pen y Fan in a **blizzard** when it cleared for our descent. This is the result of the light that transformed the scene. It was pure magic!

Apricots

drying in the sun in the Karakoram mountains.

Jamie Marshall Altit Fort, Kari, Pakistan

[*face to face*] 5

5

Jeremy Bishop Ambrym Island, Vanuatu

These men – inhabitants of Lalinda village –

helped me on and off Ambrym's vast volcanic

crater and led me through the jungle to this

waterfall

where we washed the acidic grime from our skin.

Dave Winter Karakoram highway, China

The local Kyrgyz population lives in settlements of semi-permanent **yurts** around Karakul Lake. One of my best ever travel experiences was to return the following year and present the pictures to the family.

Paul Strauson Laos

The weaver's daughter. I played hide-and-seek for some time with this shy girl until, for a fleeting moment, she appeared between these woven lengths of cloth before disappearing back into the darkness of her parents' hut.

Martin Bradley Bolivia

An Aymara girl with an alpaca on the shores of Lake Titicaca.

Roderick Macmillan Marrakesh, Morocco

Young girl in Djemaa El Fna.

After seeing her everyday for four days, she eventually let me take a photograph of her.

Chris Harrison Hoang Lien Son Mountains, North Vietnam

I was working as a voluntary research assistant with H'mong children. After school, local children of all ages helped their families on the terraced paddy fields, and they sometimes found the time to fish in the mountain streams, during the late afternoon.

Vikki Martin Mount Hagen, Papua New Guinea

A sing sing performer

takes a moment out from applying his traditional face paint before the Highlands Cultural Show begins.

Woman in the doorway of her home at a Tamil tea pickers' hill community.

Simon Spicknell Ella, Sri Lanka

I saw him sitting on the roadside and instantly warmed to him beneath his ragged hat, gently smoking.

Jenny Balfour-Paul Guizhou province, South West China

Paul Howell Tastubek, Central Kazakstan

This boy seemed particularly interested in my camera and made it his business to be in just about every picture.

Hilary Morgan Kathmandu, Nepal

I was visiting the Anandaban Leprosy Hospital when I came across three small houses, with orange or yellow washes. Both the **woman** and the **cat** looked very much at ease and fitted into their surroundings perfectly.

David Bruce Nyae Nyae Conservancy, Namibia

San hunter drinking water from an **ostrich shell.**

Jonathan Gregson Mafia Island, Tanzania

After I'd taken a fisherman's portrait he urged me to photograph his morning

catch of squid.

Sue Garfinkle Sinai, Egypt

This man and his children were selling things by the side of the road. I saw his wonderful face and was trying to get a picture before he saw me. As he noticed me I got this amazing grin from him.

During a brief road-stop, these children

appeared from nowhere,

selling postcards. Their huge eyes and intense faces

were a dream for anyone with a camera.

Bob Moore Rajasthan, India

Young girl at the Pushkar
Camel Fair.

Godfrey Talbot Orissa, India

Fisherman in the early morning at Gopalpur-on-Sea.

Eric Baldauf Todos Santos, western Guatemala

Portrait of a farmer taken

in a maize field

wearing the traditional dress of

Todos Santos, a village in the

mountains of western Guatemala.

Guy Moberly Zaria, Nigeria

Draped in yellow, this young girl looked spectacular.

Michael Ford Uzbekistan, Central Asia ●

This photo was taken on the Trans-Aral Express as we headed through Uzbekistan toward Bukhara. My fellow compartmentalists had done a bit of DIY **air-conditioning** by removing the window and just as they leaned out I clicked.

I met this horseman in Bûr Safâga where he would gallop across the sandy shores, at one with either his horse or his camel.

Chris Christoforou Red Sea coast, Egypt

Sarah McMillan Khövsgöl Nuur, Outer Mongolia

Whilst horse-trekking around Khövsgöl Lake we met this boy grazing his horses. The rural people of Mongolia are devoted to their animals.

Kevin Adlard Havana, Cuba

Elderly lady with grand-daughter near the Malecón.

Kris Allan San Juan, Pinar del Rio Province, Cuba

I'd spent the morning with the workers on a tobacco plantation at San Juan y Martinez, when this friend of theirs showed up. He was so animated and excited that I could barely understand what he was saying;

the cigar

never left his mouth.

Chris Bright Lhasa, Tibet

Tibetan woman at Dreprung Monastery. This is the second of two shots. The first had her smiling but on the second shot she pulled a face. I wasn't aware of this until I processed the film.

He was the chief of the pygmy village and told stories of hunting while others re-enacted the scenes behind him. When he finished he sat back and lit his pipe.

Tony Wilson-Bligh
Khuzi-Beiga National Park, Virunga Mountains, Zaire

The Hamer people are one of many distinct ethnic groups found in the remote Omo Valley. We were invited to a betrothal ceremony and the man pictured was one of the many colourful characters participating.

Paul Salt Omo region, Ethiopia

[brushes with nature] 6

Mike Surowiak Etosha National Park, Namibia

Zebra photographed during a tour by light aircraft of Namibia and Botswana, just before the start of the rainy season.

Rodney Griffiths Nagano, Japan

Japanese macaque, also known as the

snow monkey,

in the mountains near Nagano.

Malcolm Schuyl Nagano Prefecture, Japan

Snow monkey at Jigokudani hot springs. The photograph was taken mid-morning when the ground was covered in snow. The monkeys frequently sit in the hot springs to keep warm and groom themselves.

Simon Forrester Okonjima, Namibia

We had stopped our Landrover to get a closer look at this male cheetah when he leapt onto the bonnet. With no windscreen in place he stared at me for almost five minutes before jumping off and returning to his kill.

Jill Whillock Busanga Plains, Zambia

Mating lions, photographed on a morning game drive in the Kafue National Park.

Jenni Watson Chiefs Island, Moremi Wildlife Reserve, Botswana

For an hour the leopard relaxed with his kill but a bark from a nearby male baboon alarmed him.

In his panic he tried to move the impala which got stuck in the fork of the tree.

Caribbean **reef sharks** being fed 15 metres down at the UNEXSO shark station off Grand Bahama Island. There were about 15 sharks present during the dive, some over two metres in length.

Russell Bennett The Bahamas

Tony Ord Gulf of St Lawrence, Canada

Mother **harp seal** checking on her new-born cub on an ice floe.

Male leopard. He heard something coming from our direction and looked straight

into the lens.

Odette Gardias Central Namibia

Tony Ord Serengeti National Park, Tanzania

Family of cheetahs (mother and two almost fully grown cubs) on the lookout for prey after resting beneath a shady tree.

We were about 50 metres up a hill when I

‘shot’ this mountain lion

running against the blue sky.

Gloria Cotton Montana, USA

Stuart Collier Varanasi, India

I took a rickshaw to a bridge north of the city. The photo of these water buffalo **wallowing** in the Ganges was taken from the banks below the bridge.

John Dinham Kegalle, Sri Lanka

Baby Indian elephants **bathing** in the river at the Pinnewela Elephant Orphanage, where over sixty young elephants are free to roam the sanctuary.

Jon Hornbuckle Beni region, northern Bolivia

While walking through the forest I heard a

strange squealing noise

and found a frog struggling to escape the jaws of a tree snake

hanging from a branch.

Paul Franklin Bujumbura, Burundi

A juvenile

mountain gorilla which had been

confiscated from poachers and taken

to the Jane Goodall Institute in

Bujumbura.

Tony Ord Larsen Ice Shelf, Antarctica ●

Emperor penguins with chick **on the edge** of the Ice Shelf.

The shot was taken as the sun reached its lowest point on the horizon.

Gloria Cotton Montana, USA

We were in two feet of snow at a temperature of −21°C. The mountain lion was on the move all the time so the photography was not easy. He paused and looked back on this hilly slope.

During a truck stop under some trees in the middle of the Botswana bush, some giraffes wandered over for their **lunch** and I snapped away. I enjoyed this shot for its sheer surrealism.

[*world in motion*] 7

7

Shirley Bell Sumbawa Island, Indonesia

Buffalo racing. The Shaman stood a painted wooden doll in the river and the winner was the first cart to finish with the doll between the two buffalo.

Nigel Hall Agra, India

The boatman and the

Taj Mahal. It was a scorching 46°C day. I framed up this shot as he guided us across the waters of the Yamuna.

Raymond Jack North Pakistan

Crossing the Darkot Glacier. Light hail was falling at the time.

Tuk-tuk drivers are economical with their driving safety skills although they do consider it unlucky to run over a monk. My photographic efforts brought out the worst in our driver as he thought we were recording incriminatory evidence.

Mervyn Rees Bangkok, Thailand

Piers Newbery Jerusalem, Israel

Late afternoon, outside the **Old City walls**, near to the Jaffa Gate.

I spent ten days in the bush with **four San hunters** in the north-east of Namibia.

David Bruce Nyae Nyae Conservancy, Namibia

Jim Sherwood Vejer de la Frontera, Spain

On Easter Sunday, the streets of Vejer de la Frontera are cordoned off and two bulls are set loose to run with the youth of the town.

As the sun set on a beautifully clear day in the Thar desert, I saw this chap and his steed standing away from the crowd. There was only time for two shots before he moved off.

Keith Harris Rajasthan, India

Jenny Mackay Royal Chitwan National Park, Nepal

Whilst crossing the **Rapti River by elephant**,

this one passed the other way, transporting a weighty load of long grass for use at the base camp where the elephants are cared for.

Dorothy Burrows St Wolfgang, Austria

Paraglider

seen from the upper station of the

Schafbergbahn on a late August afternoon.

I just caught this fellow as he

raced down the street;

he seemed particularly proud of his pose.

Lawrence Worcester South India

We were travelling **upriver** to the Perfume Pagodas.

It's a tough four kilometre journey each way which the

boatwoman makes four to five times a day. I took this in a

rare moment of rest.

Steven Lee Perfume River, Hanoi, Vietnam

Giles Angel Marrakesh, Morocco

I had been standing around in the midst of the souk for quite a while, surrounded by people. For a brief moment a gap appeared and a boy came cycling towards me.

I stood at the crossroads

near the market after running

between the traffic

and smiling a lot.

Stuart Collier Ho Chi Minh City, Vietnam

Steven Lee Hanoi, Vietnam

I was simply amazed by the number of people on bicycles, motorbikes and trishaws; no cars! A cacophony of bells, hoots, whistles and clanging filled the air to warn each and every other road user.

Wanderlust

INSPIRING A PASSION FOR TRAVEL